Mauern

Photographs of Magnum Photos • Phot[...] [...]on Magnum Photos

·TERRAIL·
P H O T O

■ Editor: Jean-Claude Dubost
Desk Editor: Caroline Broué in liaison with Magnum Photos' team
Cover design: Gérard Lo Monaco and Laurence Moinot
Graphic design: Véronique Rossi
Iconographic and artistic coordination at Magnum Photos:
Marie-Christine Biebuyck, Agnès Sire, assisted by Philippe Devernay
English translation: Ann Sautier-Greening
Photoengraving: Litho Service T. Zamboni, Verona

© FINEST SA / ÉDITIONS PIERRE TERRAIL, Paris 1998
The Art Book Subsidiary of BAYARD PRESSE SA
© Magnum Photos, Paris 1998
ISBN 2-87939-170-9
English edition: © 1998
Publication number: 201
Printed in Italy

■ *Direction éditoriale : Jean-Claude Dubost*
Suivi éditorial : Caroline Broué en liaison avec l'équipe de Magnum Photos
Conception et réalisation de couverture : Gérard Lo Monaco et Laurence Moinot
Conception et réalisation graphique : Véronique Rossi
Direction iconographique et artistique à Magnum Photos :
Marie-Christine Biebuyck, Agnès Sire, assistées de Philippe Devernay
Traduction anglaise : Ann Sautier-Greening
Traduction allemande : Inge Hanneforth
Photogravure : Litho Service T. Zamboni, Vérone

© FINEST SA / ÉDITIONS PIERRE TERRAIL, Paris 1998
La filiale Livres d'art de BAYARD PRESSE SA
© Magnum Photos, Paris 1998
ISBN 2-87939-168-7
N° d'éditeur : 201
Dépôt légal : mars 1998
Imprimé en Italie

■ Verlegerische Leitung: Jean-Claude Dubost
Verantwortlich für die Ausgabe: Caroline Broué
in Zusammenarbeit mit dem Magnum Photos Team
Umschlaggestaltung: Gérard Lo Monaco und Laurence Moinot
Buchgestaltung: Véronique Rossi
Bildredaktion und grafische Gestaltung für Magnum Photos:
Marie-Christine Biebuyck, Agnès Sire; Assistent: Philippe Devernay
Deutsche Übersetzung: Inge Hanneforth
Farblithos: Litho Service T. Zamboni, Verona

© FINEST SA / ÉDITIONS PIERRE TERRAIL, Paris 1998
Der Bereich Kunstbücher von BAYARD PRESSE SA
© Magnum Photos, Paris 1998
ISBN 2-87939-169-5
Deutsche Ausgabe: © 1998
Verlegernummer: 201
Printed in Italy

"I walked around all day, my mind occupied, seeking on the streets photographs to be taken directly from life as if in flagrante delicto. I wanted above all to seize in a single image the essence of any scene that cropped up. [...] Photography is the only means of expression which freezes one specific instant", wrote Henri Cartier-Bresson, one of the founding members of the Magnum Photos Agency. During their assignments to the four corners of the earth, the photographers of this prestigious agency have all wanted to record a certain reality directly seized "from life" and to show the world as they saw and felt it. Their photographs bear witness to the experience of men, to places, times and events which their cameras have managed to capture. The personal imprint they leave on them proves, in the words of John Steinbeck, that "the camera need not be a cold mechanical device. Like the pen, it is as good as the man who uses it. It can be the extension of mind and heart...". The ambition of the series to which this album belongs is to recall the finest of these "decisive moments", where the eye of the photographer encounters the diversity of the world. Whether it is read like a report or looked at like a film, each album is above all a thematic, historic and aesthetic odyssey bringing together the best pictures from the Magnum photographers.

" JE marchais toute la journée, l'esprit tendu, cherchant dans les rues à prendre sur le vif des photos comme des flagrants délits. J'avais surtout le désir de saisir dans une seule image l'essentiel d'une scène qui surgissait. [...] De tous les moyens d'expression, la photo est le seul qui fixe un instant précis », écrivait Henri Cartier-Bresson, l'un des fondateurs de l'agence Magnum Photos. Les photographes de cette prestigieuse agence ont tous voulu, au cours de leurs reportages à travers le monde, rendre compte d'une certaine réalité « sur le vif » et montrer le monde tel qu'ils le voyaient et le ressentaient. Leurs photos témoignent de l'expérience d'hommes, de lieux, d'époques et d'événements que leur appareil a su capter. L'empreinte personnelle qu'ils laissent prouve, selon les mots de John Steinbeck, que « l'appareil-photo n'est pas nécessairement une froide mécanique. Comme la plume pour l'écrivain, tout dépend de qui la manie. Il peut être un prolongement de l'esprit et du cœur... » Restituer les plus beaux de ces « instants décisifs » au fil desquels l'œil du photographe rencontre la diversité du monde, telle est l'ambition de la collection dans laquelle s'inscrit ce livre. À lire comme un récit ou à regarder comme un film, il est avant tout une promenade thématique, historique et esthétique qui rassemble les meilleurs clichés des photographes de Magnum Photos.

DEN ganzen Tag lief ich angespannt herum, denn ich wollte in den Straßen wie auf frischer „Tat ertappte, lebensnahe Fotos machen. Vor allem hatte ich den Wunsch, in einem einzigen Bild das Wesentliche eines Geschehnisses festzuhalten [...] Von allen Ausdrucksmitteln ist die Fotografie das einzige, das einen bestimmten Augenblick fixiert", schrieb Henri Cartier-Bresson, einer der Gründer der Fotoagentur Agence Magnum Photos. Den Fotografen dieser renommierten Agentur liegt viel daran, auf ihren Reportagen in aller Welt von einer gewissen „lebensnahen" Realität Zeugnis abzulegen und die Welt so zu zeigen, wie sie sie sahen und empfanden. Die Fotos sind von ihrem Apparat eingefangene Erfahrungen mit Menschen, Orten, Zeiten und Ereignissen. Der persönliche Eindruck, die sie hinterlassen, beweist, um mit Steinbeck zu sprechen, daß „der Fotoapparat keine kalte Mechanik sein muß. Wie bei der Feder des Schriftstellers hängt alles davon ab, wer sie hält. Und manchmal ist es sogar eine Verlängerung von Geist und Gefühl ..." Die schönsten dieser „entscheidenen Augenblicke" zu zeigen, bei denen das Auge des Fotografen der Vielfältigkeit der Welt begegnet, ist die Absicht dieser Buchreihe. Wie ein Bericht zu lesen oder wie ein Film zu betrachten, ist sie vor allem ein thematischer, historischer und ästhetischer Spaziergang, auf dem die besten Bilder der Fotografen von Magnum Photos zu sehen sind.

Sergio Larrain, Peru, *Pérou,* 1960.

Raymond Depardon, Chad, *Tchad,* Tschad, 1995. | **7**

Elliott Erwitt, *France,* Frankreich, 1968. **9**

10 | Martine Franck, *France,* Frankreich, 1989.

Henri Cartier-Bresson, Spain, *Espagne,* Spanien, 1933. | **11**

Henri Cartier-Bresson, USSR, *URSS,* UdSSR, 1973.

Elliott Erwitt, Puerto Rico, *Porto Rico,* 1969.

Ernst Haas, Austria, *Autriche,* Österreich, 1945. | **15**

Harry Gruyaert, Morocco, *Maroc,* Marokko, 1988. **17**

18 | Alex Webb, Haiti, *Haïti,* 1986-1988.

Bruno Barbey, Morocco, *Maroc,* Marokko, 1985. **21**

Harry Gruyaert, Morocco, *Maroc, Marokko,* 1977. **23**

Harry Gruyaert, India, *Inde,* Indien, 1976. **25**

Henri Cartier-Bresson, *France,* Frankreich, May, *mai* 1968. **27**

Jean Gaumy, USA, *États-Unis*, 1988. **31**

James Nachtwey, *Afghanistan*, 1996. **35**

| Raymond Depardon, Federal Republic of Germany, *RFA*, Bundesrepublik Deutschland, February, *février*, Februar 1962.

James Nachtwey, Federal Republic of Germany, *RFA*, Bundesrepublik Deutschland, November, novembre 1989. **37**

| Gilles Peress, Croatia, *Croatie,* Kroatien, 1995.

Bruce Davidson, USA, *États-Unis*, 1983.

Harry Gruyaert, Belgium, *Belgique,* Belgien, 1988.

Henri Cartier-Bresson, Mexico, *Mexique,* Mexiko, 1963. **47**

Guy Le Querrec, *Ghana,* 1993. **51**

Raymond Depardon, Germany, *Allemagne, Deutschland,* 1990.

Marc Riboud, USA, *États-Unis*, 1984.

56 | Miguel Rio Branco, *Cuba,* Kuba, 1994.

Miguel Rio Branco, Spain, *Espagne,* Spanien, 1993.

Gueorgui Pinkhassov, Japan, *Japon* 1996.

Ernst Haas, USA, *États-Unis,* 1963.

James Nachtwey, 1996.

Page 36: West Berlin,
Federal Republic of Germany.
Raymond Depardon,
February 1962.
Page 36 : *Berlin-Ouest, RFA.*
Raymond Depardon,
février 1962.
Seite 36: Westberlin,
Bundesrepublik Deutschland.
Raymond Depardon,
Februar 1962.

Page 37: Vopos on the wall
near the Brandenburg Gate.
Berlin, Federal Republic of
Germany.
James Nachtwey, November
1989.
Page 37 : *Les vopos sur le mur*
près de la porte de
Brandenbourg. Berlin, RFA.
James Nachtwey, novembre
1989.
Seite 37: Vopos auf der Mauer
beim Brandenburger Tor. Berlin,
Bundesrepublik Deutschland.
James Nachtwey, November
1989.

Page 38: During the Krajina
offensive, when the Serbs left
a region where they had lived
for 400 years. A pocket of Serb
resistance presenting, at the
time the journalists arrived, all
the symptoms of a city occupied
by combatants caught between
waiting, drunkenness and
fighting. Knin, Croatie.
Gilles Peress, 1995.
Page 38 : *Pendant l'offensive*
de la Krajina, qui a vu le départ
des Serbes d'une région où ils
avaient été présents pendant
quatre cents ans. Lieu de
résistance serbe, qui, au
moment de l'arrivée des
journalistes, affichait tous les
symptômes d'une cité occupée
par des combattants pris entre
l'attente, l'ivresse et le combat.
Knin, Croatie.
Gilles Peress, 1995.
Seite 38: Krajina-Offensive

und Verlassen der Serben
einer Region, in der sie 400
Jahre gelebt hatten. Ein Ort
des serbischen Widerstands,
der bei Ankunft der
Journalisten alle Symptome
einer besetzten Stadt aufwies
und dessen Kämpfer sich in
einem Zustand des Wartens,
der Trunkenheit und des
Kampfes befanden.
Knin, Kroatien.
Gilles Peress, 1995.

Page 39: A member of a
group of Muslim fundamentalists
fleeing the Israeli army after a
demonstration in which he was
participating was dispersed.
Gaza, Israel.
James Nachtwey, December
1993.
Page 39 : *Membre d'un groupe*
de fondamentalistes musulmans
fuyant l'armée israélienne après
la dissolution d'une
manifestation à laquelle
il participait. Gaza, Israël.
James Nachtwey, décembre
1993.
Seite 39: Ein moslemischer
Fundamentalist auf der Flucht
vor der israelischen Armee
nach Auflösung einer
Demonstration, an der er
teilgenommen hatte.
Gaza, Israel.
James Nachtwey, Dezember
1993.

Page 41: The subway.
New York, USA.
Bruce Davidson, 1983.
Page 41 : *Métro à New York.*
États-Unis.
Bruce Davidson, 1983.
Seite 41: New York, U-Bahn.
USA. Bruce Davidson, 1983.

Page 42-43: Port-au-Prince,
Haiti.
Alex Webb, 1986-1988.
Page 42-43 : *Port-au-Prince,*
Haïti.
Alex Webb, 1986-1988.
Seite 42-43: Port-au-Prince,

Haiti.
Alex Webb, 1986-1988.

Page 44: The "dead rat" ball
(at the casino). Ostend,
Belgium.
Harry Gruyaert, 1988.
Page 44 : *Bal du rat mort*
(au casino). Ostende, Belgique.
Harry Gruyaert, 1988.
Seite 44: Ball der toten Ratte
(im Casino). Ostende, Belgien.
Harry Gruyaert, 1988.

Page 45: Southsea. Hampshire,
England.
Martin Parr, 1992.
Page 45 : *Southsea.*
Hampshire, Angleterre.
Martin Parr, 1992.
Seite 45: Southsea.
Hampshire, England.
Martin Parr, 1992.

Page 46-47: Puebla, Mexico.
Henri Cartier-Bresson, 1963.
Page 46-47 : *Puebla, Mexique.*
Henri Cartier-Bresson, 1963.
Seite 46-47: Puebla, Mexiko.
Henri Cartier-Bresson, 1963.

Page 48: Outside a diamond
merchant's head office.
Johannesburg, South Africa.
Ian Berry, 1984.
Page 48 : *Extérieur du siège*
d'une compagnie diamantaire.
Johannesbourg, Afrique du Sud.
Ian Berry, 1984.
Seite 48: Außenansicht
der Hauptverwaltung eines
Diamantenunternehmens.
Johannesburg, Südafrika.
Ian Berry, 1984.

Page 49: Bao Guang
monastery "of the Divine Light",
Xindu, Sichuan Province.
Inscription of the sign for good
fortune which visitors,
eyes closed, try to touch
in its centre. China.
Guy Le Querrec, 1984.
Page 49 : *Monastère Bao*
Guang, « de la divine lumière »,
Xindu, province de Sichuan.
Inscription du signe du bonheur

que les visiteurs, les yeux fer-
més, essaient de toucher en son
centre. Chine.
Guy Le Querrec, 1984.
Seite 49: Kloster
„des himmlischen Lichts"
Bao Guang, Xindu, Provinz
Sichuan. Inschrift des Zeichens
für Glück, das die Besucher mit
geschlossenen Augen in der
Mitte zu berühren suchen.
China.
Guy Le Querrec, 1984.

Page 50: Dakar, Senegal.
Marc Riboud, 1960.
Page 50 : *Dakar, Sénégal.*
Marc Riboud, 1960.
Seite 50: Dakar, Senegal.
Marc Riboud, 1960.

Page 51: Preparation
for a funeral. Mampong village,
Aburi district, Ghana.
Guy Le Querrec, 1993.
Page 51 : *Préparatifs*
pour une cérémonie de
funérailles. Village de Mampong,
district d'Aburi, Ghana.
Guy Le Querrec, 1993.
Seite 51: Vorbereitung einer
Begräbniszeremonie.
Das Dorf Mampong, Distrikt
Aburi, Ghana.
Guy Le Querrec, 1993.

Page 52: Arbat Street.
Moscow, Russia, USSR.
Carl De Keyzer, 1989.
Page 52 : *Rue Arbat. Moscou,*
Russie, URSS.
Carl De Keyzer, 1989.
Seite 52: Arbat-Straße.
Moskau, Rußland, UdSSR.
Carl De Keyzer, 1989.

Page 53: Berlin, Germany.
Raymond Depardon, 1990.
Page 53 : *Berlin, Allemagne.*
Raymond Depardon, 1990.
Seite 53: Berlin, Deutschland.
Raymond Depardon, 1990.

Page 55: New York, USA.
Marc Riboud, 1984.
Page 55 : *New York, États-Unis.*
Marc Riboud, 1984.

Seite 55: New York, USA.
Marc Riboud, 1984.

Page 56: Havana, Cuba.
Miguel Rio Branco, 1994.
Page 56 : *La Havane, Cuba.*
Miguel Rio Branco, 1994.
Seite 56: Havanna, Kuba.
Miguel Rio Branco, 1994.

Page 57: Seville, Spain.
Miguel Rio Branco, 1993.
Page 57 : *Séville, Espagne.*
Miguel Rio Branco, 1993.
Seite 57: Sevilla, Spanien.
Miguel Rio Branco, 1993.

Page 58: Broadway.
New York, USA.
Ernst Haas, 1952.
Page 58 : *Broadway.*
New York, États-Unis.
Ernst Haas, 1952.
Seite 58: Broadway.
New York, USA.
Ernst Haas, 1952.

Page 59: Wall near
the sea port. Tokyo, Japan.
Gueorgui Pinkhassov, 1996.
Page 59 : *Mur près du port.*
Tokyo, Japon.
Gueorgui Pinkhassov, 1996.
Seite 59: Mauer in der Nähe
des Hafens. Tokio, Japan.
Gueorgui Pinkhassov, 1996.

Page 61: Flaking paint.
California, USA.
Ernst Haas, 1963.
Page 61 : *Peinture écaillée.*
Californie, États-Unis.
Ernst Haas, 1963.
Seite 61: Abgeblätterte Farbe.
Kalifornien, USA.
Ernst Haas, 1963.